A SPIRIT DAUGHTER WORKBOOK

WRITTEN BY
JILL WINTERSTEEN

FOR SAGITTARIUS SEASON

NOVEMBER 21ST – DECEMBER 20TH

THE SOLAR ECLIPSE

FRIDAY, DECEMBER 3RD, 2021
11:43PM PT

SAGITTARIUS

From the waters of Scorpio we meet Sagittarius. Ruled by Jupiter and the element of Fire, the archer brings us joy, optimism, and meaning. This season is a time to enjoy life, process past events, and be hopeful for what is to come. Sagittarius Season occurs near the end of the year, when we gather with others and share beliefs, philosophies, and energy. Known as the student, the philosopher, and the wanderer, Sagittarius reminds us that everyone has something to teach us and that we can never know all there is to know in this world. If we remain open, though, to the information others provide, we can expand our consciousness through a shared collective experience.

Sagittarius inspires images of travel, including long journeys and foreign peoples. It invokes the urge to experience something novel, something unique to our senses, and something that may make us think a little differently. Sagittarius does represent wanderlust, but its deeper meaning is so much more than a trip over winter break. Sagittarius teaches us that it isn't the destination that's important, it's the journey. More importantly, it's how we face adversity and find meaning as the road twists and turns to the unexpected.

SAGITTARIUS

Sagittarius helps us view all events that occur on our paths as experiences that help us evolve. There are no negative occurrences, and there are no positive ones either. There are just energies that teach and expand us. Some may frustrate us, some may break our hearts, some may confuse us, and some may bring smiles to our faces. All the ups and downs, though, lead to one thing: expansion. It's not just about the open road or many hours at sea for Sagittarius. It's also about gaining knowledge of how the world works, the different perspectives it holds, and the higher meaning of it all.

Throughout this season, feel into what expands you. Plan a trip if you like, but more importantly, seek out new experiences with people who aren't like you. Go to a new restaurant, break up your routine, talk to someone you casually run into, and follow the signs. Another lesson of Sagittarius is to look for signs and coincidences. This energy and season are all about serendipity. In Sagittarius's eyes, a coincidence is a direct message from the Universe. If we picture the happy archer out on their journey, they are not using a road map. They leave their itinerary behind and rely on instinct, along with the signs that appear right in front of them to lead the way.

Over this season, be open to messages on your path. Be aware of your surroundings and pay attention if something seems to jump out at you. Serendipity takes many forms. It can be running into an old friend or someone who looks like an old friend. It can feel like déjà vu. It can also cause a path or direction to appear brighter, especially when you are faced with a choice. It can occur when you see the same thing over and over again. Anytime something feels like a coincidence, it's the Universe arranging itself to teach you something or give you a message. It's your job to follow and trust it.

We now come across the next lesson of Sagittarius: faith. Sagittarius encourages us to take leaps of faith even when we have no idea where we will land. Furthermore, Sagittarius wants us to take the leap and assume the best will happen. If we follow Sagittarius's philosophy that all events are meant to be and are what we need at the moment, then the best-case scenario is the one that is occurring. We never need to fear taking a step into the unknown because a silver lining can always be found in whatever outcome occurs. A higher meaning always exists for every event in the eyes of Sagittarius. As long as we're willing to look for that meaning, we can always find the lesson, growth, and magic in life.

As you journey through this season, feel where you need to take a leap. What is calling you to jump and not look back? What signs are appearing to point you in a new direction—one that may feel unfamiliar but is necessary for your evolution? Is there anything holding you back? Fear is a common response to situations that feel foreign. Notice how you handle fear in the face of novel situations over this season. Then ask yourself if you are making fear-based decisions instead of trusting your intuition. What would you do if you didn't have fear? What leap would you take?

Also, train your mind to assume the best will unfold. Know that you always rely on yourself no matter what occurs on your path. You can always make the best of any situation and find the silver lining. Furthermore, you can always find the higher meaning because it's always there waiting for your discovery. Make a commitment to yourself to always look for the deeper meaning no matter what occurs. This trust in both yourself and the Universe will help you take a needed leap of faith. Then take the journey that is calling to you and know you'll always be there to catch yourself.

NORTH NODE PLACEMENTS

This Sagittarius Season overlaps with eclipse season, a time to make great change in our lives. Eclipse seasons last for thirty-four days. This one began on November 6 and will end on December 9. It brings us a Lunar Eclipse in Taurus on November 19 and a Solar Eclipse in Sagittarius on December 3. Eclipses occur when the Sun and Moon are within 17° of a lunar node. Lunar nodes are the intersection of the Sun's path and the Moon's orbit. There is a North and a South Lunar Node. The nodes are positioned in astrological signs just like all the other planets. Currently, the North Node is in Gemini and the South Node is in Sagittarius.

Throughout eclipse season and on the eclipses, we have the opportunity to work with our personal lunar nodes. We each have nodal placements that are found in our natal charts. You can look yours up at astro-charts.com. The South Node is always directly opposite the North Node. Your South Node placement represents what you have come into this life already knowing. It shows your attachments and energies that feel familiar to you. The North Node is what you are trying to integrate and learn this lifetime. These energies feel foreign at first, and you may even resist them. Your karmic path this lifetime is to leave behind your attachments to your South Node energies and embrace your North Node's wisdom.

On an eclipse, there is tremendous potential to cut ties with your South Node and step into the power of your North Node. Throughout this eclipse season and on the Sagittarius Solar Eclipse, begin to understand and invite the energies of your North Node into your life. Notice how you might initially resist and react to them, then find ways to integrate them into your daily life. Below is a description of your North Node placements and how to work with them as you set intentions on the Solar Eclipse.

NORTH NODE PLACEMENTS

Aries North Node

Your mission this lifetime is to embrace uncertainty and stress with courage and fortitude. You benefit from situations that feel unknown, exciting, and adventurous. Anything that causes you to feel your internal fire and motivation will help you evolve into who you are meant to be. Throughout this eclipse season and Solar Eclipse, feel your passion. What excites you? Then ask yourself if you are running away from it or making it part of your life. Sometimes life needs to be less than peaceful for you to discover your strength and true willpower. Shake things up a bit and allow your internal flames to burn brightly.

Taurus North Node

Your mission this lifetime is to find peace and comfort. Your past life may have brought you many stressful or traumatic situations. This lifetime is about processing them and feeling held by those around you. Give yourself a variety of comforts when needed. Listen to your instinct. If you're tired, sleep. If you need a day off, rest. If you need a hug, ask for it. Allow yourself to connect with nature and stillness as much as possible while your energetic nerves settle. Throughout this eclipse season and Solar Eclipse, find ways to create peace in your life. Notice how you may invite, attract, or create turbulent situations in your life. Instead, choose something different. Envision yourself calm, peaceful, and held by nature. Allow your life to become easier.

Gemini North Node

Your mission this lifetime is to find and encourage conflicting perspectives. Your past life may have been full of dogmatic, one-sided thinking. This lifetime is about communicating with those around you and inquiring about how they see the world. You are here to learn and incorporate varying viewpoints. Find people who are willing to debate with you, question you, answer your questions, and talk into the wee hours. Throughout this eclipse season and Solar Eclipse, let go of any belief that feels one sided. Skip hanging out with like-minded people and find others who embrace a different perspective. Envision ways to expand your mind and curiosity as we head into the new year.

Cancer North Node

Your mission this lifetime is to heal. You need to allow yourself to cry and be held while doing it. Your past life may have brought many hardships and that didn't afford you you the ability to rest. This lifetime is about feeling safe—safe enough to let your guard down and receive love from others. Allow yourself to explore emotions and accept them as part of yourself. Throughout this eclipse season and Solar Eclipse, soften your heart and your often hard exterior. Ask for help if you need it, give yourself space to feel, and acknowledge what makes you feel safe. Envision ways you can heal your heart and hold yourself while you let your past hardships go. Life is softer this time around. Enjoy it.

Leo North Node

Your mission this lifetime is to be heard and seen. Your last lifetime brought you many insights into how the world should work. This lifetime is about sharing your unconventional thoughts and leading those around you to a new reality. Allow yourself to speak your truth and use your charismatic ways to draw in a community. Find people who will support you and help you step into your power this lifetime. Throughout this eclipse season and Solar Eclipse, feel into what you want to share with others. If you had an audience of thousands of people, what would you say to them? What is your message this life, and how will you send it out to the collective in order to lead it?

NORTH NODE PLACEMENTS

Virgo North Node

Your mission this lifetime is to help others. Your last lifetime brought you much wisdom and universal knowledge. This lifetime is about giving it to others in a way they can understand, integrate, and use to help them heal. You may initially resist this path. It takes work, dedication, and selfless acts. After all, you already hold so much wisdom. At first, you may feel content simply living your life. Your path, though, is to share what you know with those around you. Throughout this eclipse season and Solar Eclipse, envision ways you can share your knowledge with a community. Virgo is about the details. Feel into how you can give to others, then give in an organized way that helps them learn something over time. Also, feel into who can mentor you in this service. You may not require new knowledge, but you may need to be taught service. Seek out those who can help you help others.

Libra North Node

Your mission this lifetime is to find peace within yourself and in your relationships. Your past life may have brought you intense situations that caused stress and even war in your heart. This lifetime is about creating harmony around yourself. It's about choosing partners who support and ground you. It's also about noticing when you attract people who perpetuate drama or unhealthy circumstances in your life. Your goal is to feel or heal an old wound. Throughout this eclipse season and Solar Eclipse, envision people who bring you grace, ease, and support. Seek partners who feel equal. Also, create ways you can heal from your stressful past by inviting more beauty and love into your life. Connect with nature, art, music, and other things that feel good to your soul.

Scorpio North Node

Your mission this lifetime is to understand and accept your shadows. Your past life may have been filled with simplicity and lacking in psychological depth. This life invites you to dive deep into your soul and confront all aspects of yourself—even the ones you would rather ignore. Give yourself space to learn who you are through daily journaling and fierce self-inquiry. Throughout this eclipse season and Solar

Eclipse, notice when you are triggered. Instead of judging others, ask yourself what they are reflecting to you. How does the person triggering you simply serve as a mirror for one of your hidden shadows? Instead of judging yourself, accept these parts of yourself. Acknowledge the complexity of being human and envision a life that includes all parts of yourself. Turn your shadows into light by accepting them and seeing them as an asset to who you are.

Sagittarius North Node

Your mission this lifetime is to expand. Your past life may have limited you in some way to one location or one perspective when you wanted more. This life is about spreading your wings. It's about travel and long journeys to foreign lands. It's about conversations with people from different cultures. And it's about seeing the bigger picture of the world and the interconnectedness of it all. Throughout this eclipse season and Solar Eclipse, envision ways you can expand your consciousness. What is limiting you? And how can you free yourself? As we head into a new year, think about all the places you want to see and the things you want to learn this next year. How can you expand through new experiences that challenge your current reality?

Capricorn North Node

Your mission this lifetime is to focus your energy. Your past life may have involved a significant amount of healing and focus on yourself. This lifetime is about directing your attention to what is worth your energy. It's about honoring your life's mission and making it a priority. Throughout this eclipse season and Solar Eclipse, feel into what you want to focus on the most. Envision a life that grants you time and space to feel your intuition, then use it for your life's work. Commit to something that will see you through the next five or ten years and fulfill you on a soul level.

Aquarius North Node

Your mission this lifetime is to be yourself. Your past life may have been filled with people-pleasing actions as you tried to meet others' expectations. This lifetime is about doing what you want to do, even if others don't understand or approve of it. It's about deciding for yourself and no one else. Throughout this eclipse season and Solar Eclipse, notice how you allow other people's opinions to define you. How are you acting in your own life? Then envision ways you can show up as yourself. How would that feel? How would it feel if others disapproved of you? Create ways to show yourself love and acceptance, making it easier for you to digest the disapproving opinions of others.

Pisces North Node

Your mission this lifetime is to surrender and trust your enduring spirit. Your past life may have been filled with hardship and difficulty. You may even have felt like a failure in some way. This lifetime is about loving yourself and knowing that you can never fail because there is no failure. This life asks that you trust the Universe and the process of your life. You do not need to do anything. You simply need to be, and that is enough. Throughout this eclipse season and Solar Eclipse, let go of ways you invite challenges into your life. You do not need to prove yourself to anyone or to yourself. Envision a life that allows you to relax and feel the wonders of the Universe. Meditate on this Solar Eclipse and allow your intuition to reveal your next steps.

*You can look up your personal Lunar Nodes at astro-charts.com

CRYSTALS FOR SAGITTARIUS

Iolite is a wanderer's stone. It helps move you from realm to realm by aiding access to your inner compass. It can bring balance if you are feeling disoriented or lost. Iolite also helps widen your perspective by enhancing your creative side. Use some when you need to develop new ideas or want to call in new experiences. Iolite motivates you if you are feeling depleted or resistant to adventure. Take some with you when traveling. It will help you overcome days when you are feeling overwhelmed and unable to process new information. Iolite is purple.

Iolite vibrates to the mantra: "I am ready to move."

CRYSTALS FOR SAGITTARIUS

Red Jasper is both a protecting and empowering stone. It is associated with the root chakra and helps ground the wearer. It also calms the mind and clears away any emotional disturbances in the energetic body. This place of clarity allows you to claim your rightful power and move forward into the unknown. Red Jasper is a stone of luck, as many red stones are, and can bring about serendipitous interactions during your journey. Always take a piece of Red Jasper with you when traveling to call in good fortune and positive encounters. Red Jasper is reddish brown.

Red Jasper vibrates to the mantra: "I am at ease."

Aventurine is known as the stone of opportunity. It is considered one of the luckiest crystals, as it attracts opportunities to the wearer. It clears the heart of any negative vibrations, helping attract good fortune and clear vibrations. It also acts as a shield for the heart, making it a great stone in a necklace. Have some with you when you need luck and prosperity or when you feel like doors have been closing on you. It will help open doors with grace and ease. Aventurine is light green.

Aventurine vibrates to the mantra: "I am lucky."

Mookaite connects the wearer to the Earth. It creates grounding and helps plug you into the positive frequencies of Mother Gaia. It is an excellent travel companion, as it grounds you and allows for serendipity to occur on your journey. Mookaite also helps you keep a positive outlook on any adventure, even when things start to go awry. It pulls you back to center when most needed and reminds you that the Earth is always here to support you. Mookaite represents the color of the Earth with reddish-brown and beige hues.

Mookaite vibrates to the mantra: "I am grounded and ready for adventure."

Turquoise is an ancient stone of protection and nobility. It has been used for centuries in many cultures—including Native American, Egyptian, Asian, Aztec, and Inca—for its ability to protect and bring wisdom to the wearer. It's a stone of nobility and was worn by many kings and queens through the years. Go to any museum with ancient artifacts, and you will see Turquoise adorning the crowns, bracelets, and amulets of kingdoms past. Turquoise is also known as a stone of travel, protecting the wearer from the pitfalls of traveling long journeys. Carry some when embarking on an adventure, or place some in your luggage to protect against theft. Once you arrive at your destination, set the Turquoise where you can see it upon awakening. This placement will bring good luck to the rest of your day. (You can do this at home as well.) Turquoise is blue-green.

Turquoise vibrates to the mantra: "My wisdom protects me."

SAGITTARIUS MEDITATION

Sagittarius is about finding adventure and learning from it. With any great adventure, courage is the first requirement. Being courageous does not mean being fearless though. Quite the opposite. Instead, courage is cultivated through feeling fear, becoming aware of it, and not allowing it to take control. The first step in developing courage is becoming aware of your fear and acknowledging the information it carries, but not allowing it to make decisions.

The following meditation is designed to put you in touch with where fear lives in your body so you can circumvent it before it acts on your behalf. Learning about our fear in a safe, comfortable place makes us more aware of it when we are confronting new situations out in the world. Fear is an important emotion and can keep us away from truly dangerous situations, so we don't want to eradicate it completely. We just want it placed firmly in the back seat, not driving the car. Practice this meditation throughout Sagittarius Season and on her New Moon to help you learn from your fear and feel it.

Feeling Fear

Begin this meditation lying down in a comfortable position. Be in an environment that feels completely safe for you. Spend about a minute breathing deeply into your belly, exploring the rise and fall of your stomach with each breath. Concentrate your breath into your belly, not your ribs as done in other breath work. You can always return to this breathing if emotions get too intense. Breathing into your belly decreases your flight-or-fight response, which is activated during times of fear.

Allow your breath to be natural, then perform a body scan to observe the feeling from your head to your toes. Notice if there is any tension in your body or places where you cannot feel your energy circulating. Just observe without changing anything.

Now bring about a familiar feeling of fear. This feeling may be a common worry, like missing a deadline, forgetting an email, or an important person not responding to a text. Something not too intense, but a real concern in your world. Imagine it, then scan your body again. Has anything changed? Do any areas now feel tense? Can you feel fear in your body? It often feels like restriction or tension somewhere. This is the first step of awareness—to find the places in your body where fear likes to live. Once you find them, gently breathe into these areas and visualize a white light reaching them so they begin to shift and open. Do this for as long as it is comfortable for you (about five minutes or so).

Go lightly with this, so as not to rattle your nervous system too much. After you've found your fear zones, return to the deep belly breathing for five minutes, then do another body scan to see if the fear has left. If not, continue with the belly breathing.

When you're entering a new adventure, check in with these fear zones to see how they might be responding. Take charge of them before they start directing you subconsciously. Use your breath to release tension. Consciously relax the shoulders and neck, which tend to constrict when we feel confronted.

SAGITTARIUS LUNAR FLOW

Sagittarius rules the hips and thighs. This energy controls the parts of the legs and torso that help you walk or move forward. To expand into your future, you need to stretch and lengthen an area of your body called the psoas. The hip flexor is emotionally related to your fear response. When open, it allows you to walk into the unknown. When tight or constricted, it keeps you curled in a ball from fear. It's important on many energetic levels to keep this area of the body open and relaxed. The following sequence will help you release tension from this area so you are free to walk into your dreams.

Supine Apanasana/Happy Baby

Begin by lying on your back. Bend one knee and hug it into your chest. Straighten and press through the heel of your opposite leg. Take 5 breaths in your belly. Then slowly grab the inside heel of your bent leg and come into Half Happy Baby. Flex your foot and line up your ankle over your bent knee as you take your leg out to the side slightly. Take 5 belly breaths, then release to the other side. Afterward, rock about 8 times on your back up into to a seated position. From here, take a Downward-Facing Dog, peddling out your feet.

Sun Salutations with Lunges // 3 Rounds

Begin at the top of your mat in Tadasana—standing upright with your belly firm, feet pressing down, and your crown reaching toward the sky. Inhale, lift your arms to the sky. Exhale, fold forward. Inhale, lengthen out your back and look ahead. Exhale, step your right foot back for a Low Lunge. Place your right knee on the ground. On inhale, lift your arms toward the sky, spending one breath here before lowering your hands to the ground and stepping back to Plank Pose. Lower to the ground, then lift your heart for Cobra, keeping your legs on the ground. Exhale into Downward-Facing Dog. Breathe in for 5 breaths. Step your right foot forward for a Low Lunge on the other side. Your back knee rests down; on inhale, lift your arms back up to the sky. On exhale, lower your hands on either side of your foot and step your back foot forward for a fold. On inhale, lift your torso to standing, reaching your arms upward. Exhale, hands to the heart. Repeat this sequence 3 times, feeling your hips and spine begin to open. During each exhale, feel your abs activate to stabilize your core. On each inhale, breathe into your heart.

Sun Salutation B // 3 Rounds

Stand at the top of your mat. Inhale, stretch your arms overhead, and bend your knees into Chair Pose. Exhale, fold forward. Inhale, lengthen out your back. Exhale, step back into Plank Pose, and lower halfway to Chatarunga (elbows into ribs). Inhale, reach your chest up for Upward-Facing Dog, with everything off the ground except your hands and feet. Exhale, Downward-Facing Dog Pose (this sequence is also known as a Vinyasa). Inhale, step your left foot forward to Warrior 1. With your back foot flat on the ground at a 45° angle, bend into your front knee and lift your arms to the sky. Take 5 breaths here, opening into your back leg as you tilt your tailbone to the ground. Exhale, release into Plank. Lower to Chaturanga. Inhale into Upward-Facing Dog. Exhale, Downward-Facing Dog. Repeat on the right side, then remain in Downward-Facing Dog for 5 breaths. Exhale, step to the top of the mat. Inhale, lengthen through your spine. Exhale, fold forward. Inhale, Chair Pose. Exhale, hands to heart. Breathe at the top of your mat as you feel your energy circulating throughout your body.

Warrior 2 > Reverse Warrior > Triangle > Half Moon

Step your feet 3 to 4 feet apart. Turn your left foot forward with your back foot at a 45° angle. Bend deeply into your front knee for Warrior 2. Reach your arms out to both sides and look forward. Firm your back leg to open your hip even more as you draw your lower belly in, tilting your tailbone to the ground. Spend 5 breaths here. On exhale, flip your front palm up to the sky and tilt back for Reverse Warrior, arching your arm overhead and stretching your torso back. Stay bent in your front knee, opening through your side. Feel the play between opening your torso and bending your knee. Take 5 breaths here, breathing into your side waist. On inhale, reach your torso up and straighten your front knee. Upon exhale, hinge forward, folding over your front leg for Triangle. Rotate your chest toward the right and reach your right arm up to the sky. Press firmly through your back leg, keeping your lower abs engaged. Take 5 breaths here, rotating a little bit more on every exhale. Slowly look down at the ground and come into Half Moon Pose. Place your left hand on the floor outside your left foot. You can use a block here to lift the floor up to you. Lift your right leg up, balancing on your left. Flex your right foot and rotate your torso toward the sky, reaching your left arm up. Gaze at your left hand and take 5 breaths, pressing through your back heel. Slowly place your left foot down. Inhale, reach your torso upright, and turn your feet so that your right foot is facing forward. Repeat on the other side. After your second side, bring your feet parallel and fold over your straight legs. Place your arms to the ground. Allow your spine and neck to fully decompress as you take 5 breaths here. Inhale, slowly come back to standing and return to the top of your mat.

Lizard Pose > Half Splits Pose

Step back into Plank Pose, then take a Downward-Facing Dog, peddling out your feet. From Downward-Facing Dog, step your left foot outside your left hand. Lower your back knee down and sink your hips forward. Feel the front of your right thigh opening as you breathe. If you'd like to go deeper, you can lower to your elbows. After 5 breaths, bring your front foot back in line with your front hip. Straighten that leg out for Half Splits Pose. Have your hips directly over your back knee and fold forward over your straight leg. Use blocks under your hands if you need to and keep your back as straight as possible as you fold. After 5 breaths, return to Downward-Facing Dog and switch sides.

Pigeon Pose

Return to Downward-Facing Dog through a Vinyasa or by stepping back. Then take your left knee to your left wrist for Pigeon Pose. Be gentle with your knee. If you feel any pain, do Thread the Needle Pose, which is a Pigeon modification. Carefully lay down your left leg and stretch your right leg back. Before folding, press up through your hands and arch your back a bit, extending through the front of your body. On exhale, fold forward over your leg and remain here for 10 breaths. On each inhale, send your breath into your hips, encouraging them to open. On exhale, release a bit more. After 10 breaths, slowly switch sides.

Savasana

Release onto the floor, lying with your palms up and eyes closed. Feel your body alive with the circulation of new energy.

ALIGNING THE SPIRIT

TIPS FOR MANIFESTING YOUR DREAMS

I SEE MY LIFE AS AN UNFOLDING SET OF OPPORTUNITIES TO AWAKEN

— RAM DASS

Sagittarius Season helps us feel that our dreams are possible and attract the energy we need to manifest them. It reminds us that the best-case scenario will always unfold and our job is to trust the process of our lives. Over Sagittarius Season, it's possible to truly embody some of the founding principles of the law of attraction. The law states that we are energetic beings and the energy we emit attracts the energy we encounter in our lives. Our thoughts create our reality. It's possible to change our lives through changing our thoughts, behavior, and energy.

As we work with the energy of the Universe and the law of attraction, it's important to note that we are co-creating with the Universe. We clearly define what we want in our lives and expect it to occur. Over this season, experiment with different techniques that help communicate your dreams to the Universe while you know that those dreams will always occur. Expect these things to become your reality, then watch them manifest. There is a lot of work to do on yourself to become clear in your energy and let go of your blocks, but you can do the work. It just takes commitment and resolve. Below are some tips for working with this Sagittarius Season as you begin to feel your manifestation powers.

Own Your Dreams
The first step in manifesting your dreams is to define them. Become crystal clear on what you want, then own it. Admit to yourself and others your biggest dreams. Notice if you don't feel worthy or if you have initial doubts when first speaking your dreams. Know that you are worthy of them and that by simply declaring your desires, you are telling the Universe that you are ready to have them in your life.

Write Your Dreams
Write down your dreams every day on paper. Begin by writing them on the New Moon through intention-setting, then write a few statements each day that reaffirm your dreams. You can write them two, three, or even thirty times each day. The more you write them, the more you will affirm to the Universe that you are ready to receive them.

Let Go of Resistance
It's natural to have resistance to your dreams. Dreams require change, and change is scary. As you write and speak your dreams, notice parts of your body that may tense up or thoughts that pop up in your mind. Address these thoughts and tensions with deep breaths and acceptance. Have a conversation with your fears and doubts, and ask what they are really about. Learn from them and reassure yourself that you are ready for your dreams. You are ready for the changes you desire.

Create a Worry Journal
It's natural for worries and what-ifs to pop up when you dream big. You may wonder

what will happen if you fail or how your friends will treat you. You may even wonder if you'll lose yourself once your dreams manifest. Dedicate a journal to all of your worries. Once a day, write down all the concerns that come up when you envision your dreams manifesting. Acknowledge them and learn from them, but do not allow them to control your thoughts. Simply say to them, "I hear you, but I am not going to allow you to interfere with my power."

Move Your Energy
When creating big shifts in your energy and life, it's important to move through exercise. Yoga is an excellent method for breaking up stagnant energy, but so are other forms of exercise. Mediation is also excellent for helping calm your mind and worries. It can move your energy subtly, and that subtle shift may be all you need to change the energy you emit.

Write Down Small Steps
Write down something you can do each day to help manifest your dreams. As you complete these actions, you will know that you have control of your destiny and are co-creating your dreams with the Universe. This confidence will reaffirm that you are ready for your dreams.

Become Your Future Self
Think like your future self—the one who has already manifested their dreams. What would they do? What would they say? Embody this energy and become this person. Once you can fully think of yourself as having already manifested your dreams, they will become more possible.

Speak as If It's Already Happened
When you talk about your dreams, speak as if they are already real. Some people may look at you little funny, but that's ok. You're the one who will soon be living the reality you speak into existence.

Feel Your Dreams
Along with speaking about your dreams, feel as if they have already happened. Then ask yourself how you feel about it. Hold this feeling as you work on manifesting your dreams. Hold the feeling of them already being real.

Believe
Believe your dreams can occur—because they can! Notice when you start to lose belief and bring yourself back to your intentions. Read your writings and embody the feeling of your dreams.

Trust the Process
Manifesting your dreams sometimes means being patient and trusting the process. You may not always understand why something is, or isn't, occurring, but don't let that make you lose faith in your manifestation powers. Keep holding the vision, writing your dreams, and noticing the signs that come up on your path. Do the work to remove the blocks within you and trust that everything is unfolding how it needs to for your evolution. Trust that every twist and turn is meant to be, and keep believing that you can manifest any vision.

Be Grateful
Gratitude always attracts more things to be grateful for. Practice gratitude every day, even for the smallest of things. Be grateful for the signs you receive, the encouragement that comes your way, and yourself for believing in your power to dream.

SOLAR ECLIPSE

DECEMBER 3RD

On the Sagittarius New Moon, we have a Total Solar Eclipse. This eclipse can be seen from Antarctica, but its effects will be felt everywhere. The eclipse begins at 11:00 p.m. Pacific time on December 3. It reaches its maximum at 11:33 p.m. Pacific time and ends at 12:06 a.m. Pacific time on December 4. Solar Eclipses occur on New Moons, while Lunar Eclipses occur on Full Moons. They are powerful energetic portals we can walk through to shift long-standing patterns and change our lives in the blink of an eye. Solar Eclipses are essentially supercharged New Moons. They bring us all the magic of a New Moon, but amplified. They create a pathway for release but also strengthen our intuition and resulting intentions.

SOLAR ECLIPSE

DECEMBER 3RD

We have two or three Solar Eclipses a year that are part of two annual eclipse seasons. What makes them possible is the Moon and Sun's proximity to the lunar nodes. The North and South Lunar Nodes exist where the Sun's path and the Moon's orbit intersect. They are energetic vortices full of magic and potential. When the Moon and Sun meet near a lunar node, we have a Solar Eclipse. Lunar nodes are also called the Nodes of Fate. They determine the fate of our personal karmic journeys and the journey of society from one cycle to the next. When we add the lunar nodes' energy into the already potent New Moon energy, we feel our destiny and power to create it. We also feel what blocks our journeys and what we need to release to step up to the next level of our lives.

Just like the Moon and Sun, the North and South Nodes are located within a zodiac constellation. Currently, the North Node is located in Gemini, while the South Node sits oppositional in Sagittarius. This eclipse occurs as the Moon and Sun meet near the South Node in Sagittarius. This meeting at the South Node on a New Moon gives us a feeling of release and letting go that is normally associated with a Full Moon. The Sun and Moon illuminate what we need to release to step into our power and embrace our potential. We also can see what aspects and energies of Sagittarius are showing up in our lives and blocking our paths forward. We can then release them and open the doorway for new energies to enter.

The South Node represents what we are leaving behind as a society, particularly the sign's lower vibrations. It is what the collective is evolving away from and often shows us vibrations we have already mastered as a society. The South Node in Sagittarius asks us to step away from self-righteousness and judgment. It illuminates places where we have aligned with these energies and inspires us to look within instead of outwardly. When we judge others, we often are projecting a self-judgment. Instead of accepting that we are embracing the energy we are judging, we project it onto others in efforts to make ourselves feel better and more in control.

Through withdrawing projections, we can accept a new truth that we are not perfect and do not know everything. We are not all-knowing, and that's ok. We are still students of the Universe and will still make mistakes as we continue to learn. In this new truth, we can let go of judgments of others and self-righteousness as we accept that we are human. This Solar Eclipse in Sagittarius invites us to open our minds and envision a new world where we seek to learn from differing viewpoints. It helps us understand the interconnectedness of all beings instead of judging others or projecting our self-judgments onto them.

On this Solar Eclipse, we have the opportunity to make energetic leaps through releasing the lower frequencies of Sagittarius and understanding how it helps us embrace our personal North Node frequencies discussed in a previous section of this workbook. When you find out your personal North Node, ask yourself how the highest vibrations of Sagittarius can help you integrate the energies of your North Node into your life. This may include shifting the way you view things, releasing judgment of yourself or others, or simply admitting you don't know everything. Additionally, ask whether focusing on the best-case scenario can help you embrace the lessons of your personal North Node. This Solar Eclipse is still a New Moon. It carries with it all the potential for new beginnings. Embrace a new version of yourself—one that includes the vibrations of your North Node.

SAGITTARIUS SOLAR ECLIPSE

DECEMBER 3RD

This Solar Eclipse brings us the last New Moon energy of 2021. New Moons are about beginnings and the seeds of intentions. This one, though, carries an element of release and finality. As the Sun meets the Moon, it reveals everything we are ready to say goodbye to in these last days of 2021. As we detach from these energies, beliefs, and actions, we clear the way for new vibrations to shape our lives and the next year. This eclipse also gives us the opportunity to find meaning in the past year and all the events it has brought us. It's a time to reflect upon what we have learned and how this knowledge has helped us evolve. Perhaps this evolution did not come easy or with approval, but it was necessary to shape us into the people we are meant to be.

SAGITTARIUS SOLAR ECLIPSE

DECEMBER 3RD

As you journey through this Solar Eclipse New Moon, give yourself space to pause and look back at the past year. What has it taught you? What gifts did it bring? What are you ready to process and find meaning in? Also look at the stories you tell yourself about what has occurred this year and in years past. We hold many ongoing narratives that form our internal truths. We tell ourselves stories about what we have experienced. These narratives affect our energy and our truths. They form our identities, our mantras, and our perspectives of the future. Some of these truths are positive and encourage our growth, while some are negative and limit our potential.

Over this eclipse, listen to the stories you tell yourself. The Sun and Moon sit next to Mercury in Sagittarius, making this an excellent time to journal and ask yourself questions to develop your understanding. What narratives define your world? How do you see yourself in these stories? Are you focusing on the positive aspects and silver linings, or are you focused on the drama and negativity? Rewrite the stories you tell yourself about the past and the people in your life. You may not be able to change the past, but you can change the story you tell yourself about it. When you change your perspective, you change your energy. You may even find healing and detachment as you process the same event though a different narrative.

As you rewrite your old stories and set new intentions, focus on hope and positivity. This Solar Eclipse is a powerful event. Coupled with Sagittarius, it brings optimism and joy. It's a time to look for the best-case scenario and assume it will happen. It's also a time to recognize how and when you doubt the best-case scenario. What has shaped your perspective of the future? Do you allow yourself to think positively and know the best will unfold? Or do you doubt the serendipity and support of the Universe? More importantly, do you doubt your ability to create a life full of positivity and alignment?

Also look at the ways you limit yourself when writing your intentions. We often hold back our true dreams for fear of failure. We don't allow ourselves to step into our full power and or even to admit what the heart truly wants. Part of this self-limiting behavior comes from the fear of change. We tend to cling to the familiar even if it makes us unhappy or feel less than fulfilled. Stepping into our highest visions often requires big changes and new experiences. It also asks that we take on new stories and perspectives. These changes can feel scary, and we react by limiting our dreams and requests of the Universe.

Over this eclipse, look at the ways you limit yourself. Is there a dream you are resisting because it feels too big? Do you self-sabotage right at the precipice of breaking through to a new level of existence? This Solar Eclipse works with the energy of Jupiter, Sagittarius's ruling planet. Jupiter asks us to expand and feel our true potential. It asks us to look at how we sell ourselves short and why. As you work with this energy, feel into your full potential, then ask yourself if it scares you. If it does, know that it's ok. Our full potential is often a lot to digest and process. Feel into all of your dreams, then challenge yourself to dream bigger. What would it feel like to live in your full potential? Who would you be if you let go of the fear? Who would you be if you allowed yourself to grow into who you're capable of becoming? Then envision this person and invite them into your world to teach you, help you grow, and inspire you to take a leap toward your biggest dreams and brightest visions.

SETTING UP FOR MAGIC

FOR YOUR ALTAR OR MOON CIRCLE

FLOWERS:
Bamboo, Carnation, Jade,
Narcissus, Holly, Dandelion

COLORS:
Purples (Deep & Royal),
Raspberry

TEXTURES/FABRIC:
Leather, Bamboo

SCENTS:
Cinnamon, Clary Sage, Vanilla,
Frankincense

SHAPES:
Pentagon

ELEMENTS:
Candles, Outdoor Fire

The energy of a Solar Eclipse can feel a bit chaotic. When getting ready to set intentions with this energy, it's important to choose a space that feels steady, safe, and connected to nature. If possible, practice your eclipse ritual outside by a body of water, near the forest, or somewhere you can feel the Earth below you. If this is not available to you, bring some elements of nature into your space.

SETTING UP FOR MAGIC

Set up your space much like you would for a New Moon circle. Have all of the elements present. For an eclipse, create a large crystal grid in the center of your space that will help anchor the energy. This grid can be made of tumbled stones, other crystals, flowers, seashells, or even pieces of nature you've collected on a walk. Build your grid with the four directions. Place a candle or larger crystal at the East, South, West, and North points. Place a large crystal sphere, or generator, in the center of the grid, then intuitively fill in the rest. If you are practicing with a group of people, they can sit around the grid, with the person leading the circle facing the eastern point. If you are practicing alone, face East. The East ushers in new wisdom and is the energetic home of the New Moon and Solar Eclipse.

You can incorporate the crystals suggested for Sagittarius into your space. Additionally, you can use Clear Quartz, Orange Selenite, or Lemurian, which are excellent energies for an eclipse. Crystals represent the Earth element. Include candles for the Fire element or build fire outside. Have Water near you in a metal bowl, vase, or other dish for this element. For the Air element, use essential sprays, a room diffuser, or even wind chimes to hear the air around you. Combine the additional elements for Sagittarius any way you like, including them in your circle or altar.

Once you have your space ready, cleanse it and yourself with sustainably harvested palo santo. Go around the room in a clockwise direction, starting in the East, allowing the smoke to waft to every corner. Make sure to open a window if you are indoors to allow the energy to release. If you are outside, go around the perimeter of your circle with smoke, envisioning a white circle. You can then cleanse yourself by wafting the smoke around your body from head to toe, making sure to cover the soles of your feet. Feel the unwanted energy leave your field and return to Mother Earth to be composted.

After your space is set up and cleansed, ground yourself by closing your eyes and feeling the Earth beneath you. Connect with the sensation of the Universe holding and supporting you. Take a few deep breaths with your eyes closed and merge your energy with the energy of the cosmos. As you open your eyes, take in the energy of the space. If you feel overwhelmed at any point, steady your energy by focusing on the space supporting you.

Practice the yoga and meditation in this workbook to further ground your energy. When you feel centered in your power, perform an eclipse releasing ritual. Write down energies you no longer want in your life. These can be emotions you are ready to release or stories you no longer wish to carry. Write freely, allowing your consciousness to dump on the paper. When you've finished, close your eyes and hold the piece of paper in front of your face. Inhale into your chest. As you exhale, imagine the energy you want to release leaving your field and landing on the paper. Repeat this breath three times. Open your eyes and take the paper to the fire. Burn the page in a metal dish or another safe container. You may also burn it in an outside fire. Watch the page go up in flames and turn into ashes. Watch your energy transform in front of you. If possible, collect some of the ashes from the burnt paper. Place them in the bowl of water with a Clear Quartz crystal to be further cleansed. This final step is not needed for release, but it can help enhance the ritual. Let the water sit for twenty-four hours, then throw it in a larger body of water or down the drain.

After you've performed the releasing ritual, continue with the practices in this workbook. Answer the questions and write your intentions, feeling the eclipse bring in an abundance of new energy for you to harness.

Lessons from Sagittarius:

- never stop expanding.

- magic is everywhere if you dare to look.

- alignment is a natural state of being.

- it's all unfolding as it's meant to be.

- spirit daughter

SOLAR ECLIPSE QUESTIONS

These questions are designed to help you become clear in your intentions. Take a few deep breaths to ground yourself before answering them. Sit with each question for a moment and allow the answer to naturally arise, being open to the person you are becoming. As you write, know you are opening the door to your intuition and giving permission to your highest visions to come out and be seen.

1. What signs or messages have appeared to help you write your intentions?

_____

_____

_____

_____

_____

_____

_____

_____

_____

_____

2. What do you need to release to unlimit yourself and step into your full potential?

_____

_____

_____

_____

_____

_____

_____

_____

_____

_____

3. How do you find the higher meaning and silver linings in past events?

_____

_____

_____

_____

_____

_____

_____

_____

_____

_____

_____

4. What leap do you need to make? What's the best that can happen?

_____

_____

_____

_____

_____

_____

_____

_____

_____

_____

_____

INTENTION SETTING

Today is the last New Moon of 2021. Coupled with the Solar Eclipse, it is a powerful time to envision the future, including your first months of 2022. While you don't need to know everything you want to call in next year, this eclipse is an opportunity to shed what you don't want and align your vision toward what you desire. Solar Eclipses are potent times for sending out amplified intentions to the Universe through our visions. The first step in this process is to understand what blocks your visions and expansion. Use this time to see beyond your self-imposed limitations and step out of your comfort zones. If you set intentions around the same energies month after month, try venturing into something different. Write intentions around something you've never considered and allow your dreams to expand into new territory.

Feel into the transformation you have undergone this year. Acknowledge how you have changed this last year and how you've evolved. Know that you are different person from who you were last year at this time, and have gratitude for all the events that have shaped this version of yourself. Write your intentions for this current version, and notice if you've been writing for someone who no longer exists. Create intentions for who you are today and who you are willing to become.

This eclipse also the last eclipse on the Sagittarius/Gemini axis for many years. Next month, the nodes move to Taurus and Scorpio, bringing us a new set of energies to work with on eclipses. Reflect upon how you have changed in these last eighteen months while the nodes have been in Gemini and Sagittarius. What is coming up for you that is reminiscent of last December, this past May, or May 2020? What do you need to reprocess and release? Who are you now and what aspects of yourself have evolved through these months? As you review your intentions, write them down to help you step into the next cycle of your life. Write them to honor the path you have traveled and the steps you are now ready to take.

On the Sagittarius Solar Eclipse, it's beneficial to write intentions around taking leaps into the unknown. Suspend fear and ask yourself what's the best that can happen. Allow this positivity to drown out any what-ifs or self-doubts when writing your intentions. Feel how this positive vibration and outlook can help you attract serendipity, flow, and the impossible into your life. Resist the urge to limit yourself in any way and know that you are ready to step into your full potential. Before even picking up the pen, say to yourself, "I am ready to step into my full potential."

Then close your eyes and feel that person. Feel your full potential and see this person in the future. You can envision a month ahead, six months ahead, or years ahead. See yourself standing in your power and walking through your life. As if you are watching a movie, see the details of your future life unfold in front of you. What are you doing? Who are you talking with? Where are you? What does it feel like? What does your heart feel? Continue to create this scene in your mind. Know that everything you are watching is already yourself. All you desire to change has already occurred. Do not worry about how you will get there or the list of to-dos needed to accomplish your goals. Just focus on the feeling of already living your dream. Know with every ounce of your being that it already exists for you. Also, know that your intuition, not your logic, will lead you to this dream.

Write in as much detail as possible, and write without limits. Just let your mind explore. Align with the energy of Sagittarius to clarify your dreams. How are you going to own the story of your life? How are you going to stay positive in the face of any storm that may come your way? As you write, feel a sense of gratitude for what you are dreaming, thank the Universe for giving it to you, and thank yourself for creating it. Gratitude always creates abundance.

INTENTION SETTING

VISION BOARD

Sagittarius is all about seeing the bigger picture of your life. This vision includes your hopes and dreams, and the truths you live by. One way to envision your dreams is to create a vision board. Vision boards help you see your intentions. They hold space for your dreams and give you something to return to visually when you doubt yourself and become lost in your life. Gather images that inspire you and help you believe that your dreams are possible. These images can be from any source as long as they help you hold the vision of your best life. You can use magazines, print-outs, or even images of people you know who inspire you. After you've collected pictures of your dreams, create a vision board or a dream collage. You can create a physical board with paper, cutting out images from a magazine or other source. You can also create a digital vision board using images you've collected from digital sources. Just make sure that no matter what type of board you create, you can refer to it daily to inspire and motivate you toward your dreams.

Sagittarius

BOLD. EXPANSIVE. SPONTANEOUS. LIVELY.

Sagittarius Sun:

People with their Sun in Sagittarius are generally the life of the party. They are extroverted and quick witted, and they light the room up with their smile. They seek freedom at all costs and define the meaning of wanderlust. They have a deep desire to discover the world and learn about different cultures. They also tend to throw caution to the wind and hope for the best. Life consistently rewards them for their trust by bringing them serendipitous encounters and signs if they are willing to pay attention to them.

Aligned with their high side, Sagittarius Suns have an open mind that is ready to absorb new information. They put experiences above everything else in their life and see the beauty in different places, people, and ideas. They understand that not everything may go according to plan but what does unfold is the best scenario for their evolution. After gathering new perspectives, they bring their knowledge back to their community and become the benevolent professor. They have a natural love of teaching and understand that they are both the teacher and the student in every situation.

When Sagittarius aligns with the lower vibration of their Sun energy, they embody the energy of righteousness, assuming that their knowledge is superior because it is vast. They also are prone to existential crises, forgetting to find a higher meaning in life. Sagittarius Suns are prone to contemplating the purpose of themselves and the world around them. In their low side, they begin to wonder what it's all for and doubt the meaning of everything.

In order to balance themselves, it's best for a Sagittarius Sun to find new experiences that challenge them to learn something. It's also essential for them to feel inspired by the world around them, which may mean traveling to foreign lands to learn from others. Most importantly, Sagittarius Suns need to search for the silver linings in every situation. They must trust that there is a bigger picture and be willing to take a leap to find it.

Sagittarius Moon:

People with their Moon in Sagittarius crave freedom. They are very positive, like Sagittarius Suns, spreading cheer everywhere they roam. They prefer to remain flexible in their emotions. They shy away from commitment and often choose the open road over the usual anchors. However, they can form deeply committed relationships with partners who crave freedom as much as they do.

Sagittarius Moons love traveling and living with others, as they love sharing experiences with others. They have no tolerance, though, for drama or games. They would rather be alone than deal with anyone dampening their vibe. When paired with the right people, they treasure the ability to enjoy the world with those willing to explore it with them.

Sagittarius Moons can feel depressed if their choices are limited. Travel is often an excellent remedy, but creating an unconventional life is a better long-term solution. This Moon Sign needs variety and will end up feeling trapped if life becomes redundant. When they stay focused on the bigger picture, though, life becomes a series of adventures, each one leading to expansion.

ASTROLOGY FORECAST

NOVEMBER 24TH - DECEMBER 19TH

Nov. 24: Mercury Enters Sagittarius

Mercury joins the Sun in the expansive vibrations of Sagittarius today. Mercury's time in Sagittarius expands us through communication. It's a time to exchange energies with others and learn from them. In Sagittarius, Mercury provides the opportunity to process ideas and concepts at a rapid rate. Be open to new information and energetic downloads, and listen to others when they tell their stories.

ASTROLOGY FORECAST

NOVEMBER 24TH - DECEMBER 19TH

Nov. 27: Last Quarter in Virgo

This Last Quarter is an opportunity to completely let go of energy that no longer serves our inner Goddess. Tonight's Moon in Virgo asks you to heal any part of you that does not feel in control of your life. Along with the Moon, you have the Sun in Sagittarius asking you to expand to your greatest potential. What prevents you from fully stepping into your power and realizing you are the director of your life? What part needs healing, love, and nurturing for you to grasp your potential? And are there any resistances in your energy preventing you from fully letting go of what you need to?

Dec. 1: Neptune Direct in Pisces

Today Neptune stations direct, activating the energy of this planet. Spend time with your dreams today, and be open to visions that come through your imagination. Allow your mind to wander and be curious about where it goes when undirected.

Dec. 10: First Quarter in Pisces

Today the First Quarter Moon lands in Pisces, reminding you to trust the flow of your life, even if it seems confusing at times. The path to your dreams is not always a straight journey. It takes twists and turns that don't make sense at the moment. It is full of "mistakes" or "missteps" that you'll later label as lessons. It requires you to let go of what you think should happen, embrace what is happening, and trust that everything is unfolding perfectly.

Dec. 13: Mercury Enters Capricorn

When Mercury enters Capricorn, your communication becomes grounded both with yourself and others. Your thoughts slow down a bit, and what you want to say becomes crystal clear. This transit is a great time to journal and ask yourself the harder questions about what you are manifesting. It brings details to your intentions and allows you to gain clarity on your soul's true desires. With this transit occurring over the new year, it brings the opportunity to create decisive intentions for the future.

Dec. 19: Venus Retrograde in Capricorn

Venus stations retrograde in Capricorn today until January 29. Venus stations retrograde every eighteen months for forty days. The last time it stationed retrograde in Capricorn was at the end of 2013. This current retrograde may bring up issues from eight years ago around matters of the heart. Consider this time an opportunity to find closure, heal, and reprocess old events. You may even just find yourself reliving an old story of the heart or running into an old love. Know this encounter may not be an invitation to rekindle a romance, but it may be just the opportunity you need to break an energetic tie and move forward in your life with a clear heart.

While you may not experience a reemergence of a love from 2013, Venus Retrograde brings an opportunity to assess what you really love in life. It also asks you to look at how you express your love to yourself and others. Throughout this period of Venus Retrograde, feel into what truly inspires love in your being. What taps you into your heart and reminds you of the beauty known to this world? What opens you to connect with others and feel universal love coming through you?

CAPRICORN SEASON

DECEMBER 21ST

Capricorn's energy greets us just in time for the new year. This energy both steadies us and guides us in making pivotal steps towards our visions and goals.

HAPPY
SOLAR ECLIPSE!

Thank you to everyone who supported and purchased this workbook.

Special Thanks to Rebecca Reitz (rebeccareitz.com, @becca_reitz) for her beautiful artwork on the cover, page 2, 4, 6, 10, 18, 28, 30.

For a monthly subscription contact hello@spiritdaughter.com or visit www.spiritdaughter.com.

Follow along our journey on IG:
@spiritdaughter

We always love seeing your photos & hearing about your experiences with the workbooks! Tag us to be featured on our community page:
@spiritdaughtercollective